What's Best for Red?

Casey Eggers
Illustrations by Sally Springer

HAMPTON-BROWN

"Let's plant a garden," said
Mr. Taft one day to his class. "And
let's plant in groups. Group I can grow
something yellow. Group 2 can grow
something blue. Group 3 can grow
something pink. And the last group,
Group 4, can grow something red."

The groups could not wait to start.

Group 1 wanted to grow marigolds.

Group 2 wanted to grow Johnny-jump-ups.

Group 3 wanted to grow snapdragons.

But the last group did not know what to grow.

"Let's grow something we can eat," said Cass.

"Yes, let's grow something we can use to make red jam and red pie," said Rusty.

"Let's grow something that grows fast," said Matt.

"But what?" asked Jill.

"How about beets?" said Matt.
"Beets are red and you can eat them.
Why don't we grow beets?"

"Beets do not pass the taste test,"
said Cass. "Think of beet jam—yuck!
Think of beet pie—yuck!"

"Let's not grow beets," said Matt.

"How about cherries?" said Rusty. "Cherries are red, and cherries taste great. Cherries make great jam and pie. Mr. Taft, can we grow cherries?"

"Cherries grow on trees," said Mr. Taft. "And trees take a long time to grow."

"Let's not grow cherries!" said Rusty.

"How about raspberries?" said Cass. "Raspberries are red. Raspberries make great jam and pie. And raspberries don't grow on trees, do they?"

"Raspberry plants have big thorns," said Mr. Taft. "And raspberries take a long time to grow, too."

"Let's not grow raspberries!" said Cass.

"Hey, how about strawberries?"
said Jill. "Strawberries are red.
Strawberries make great jam and pie.
And strawberries grow fast, too.
Mr. Taft, can we grow strawberries?"
"Yes, you can!" said Mr. Taft.

The next day, Mr. Taft gave the
group some strawberry plants. Cass,
Rusty, Matt, and Jill put each plant in
the damp, soft dirt.

"Stamp on the dirt to get rid of the
bumps," said Matt.

Then they gave the plants lots
and lots of water.

Weeks went by. The plants got big and green. Then came lots of blossoms. The blossoms turned into little lumps. Then the lumps got big and green.

"I don't see any red yet," said Cass.

"Soon," said Mr. Taft. "Very soon."

At last, the green lumps turned red!
"Here's something red at last!"
yelled Rusty.

Soon Cass, Rusty, Jill, and Matt
were picking strawberries.

They picked enough strawberries for jam. And they picked enough strawberries for pie. And they had enough strawberries left to eat all they wanted.

But look! The strawberry plants
were not just growing strawberries.
They were growing more plants, too!
Soon, there would be many more
strawberries, and lots more red!